ROOTED IN
Sweetness

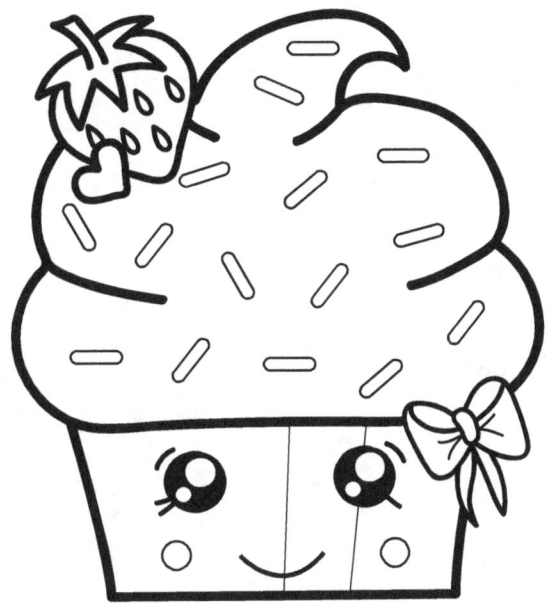

A coloring adventure for all

Jeanette Wummel

Coloring Tip:

When coloring with markers place a piece of paper between pages to prevent bleeding to your next design.

Acknowledgments

I can never say thank you enough to all the people who have supported and encouraged me in making my dreams come true. I would like to give a big thank you to my fans. I love hearing from you all. You all inspire me and make me want to keep creating! Keep being awesome!

Follow me

Website/Blog:
www.TheRootsofDesign.com

Facebook:
www.facebook.com/TheRootsofDesign

Facebook Group:
www.facebook.com/group/ColoringRoots

Instagram:
www.instagram.com/therootsofdesign

Twitter:
https://twitter.com/Roots_Of_Design

Etsy:
www.RootsDesign.Etsy.com

Patreon:
www.patreon.com/RootsOfDesign

Copyright

Published and Manufactured in the United States
www.TheRootsOfDesign.com

Designs: Jeanette Wummel

ISBN-10: 0-9982152-4-4
ISBN-13: 978-0-9982152-4-2

This Book Belongs To:

_____

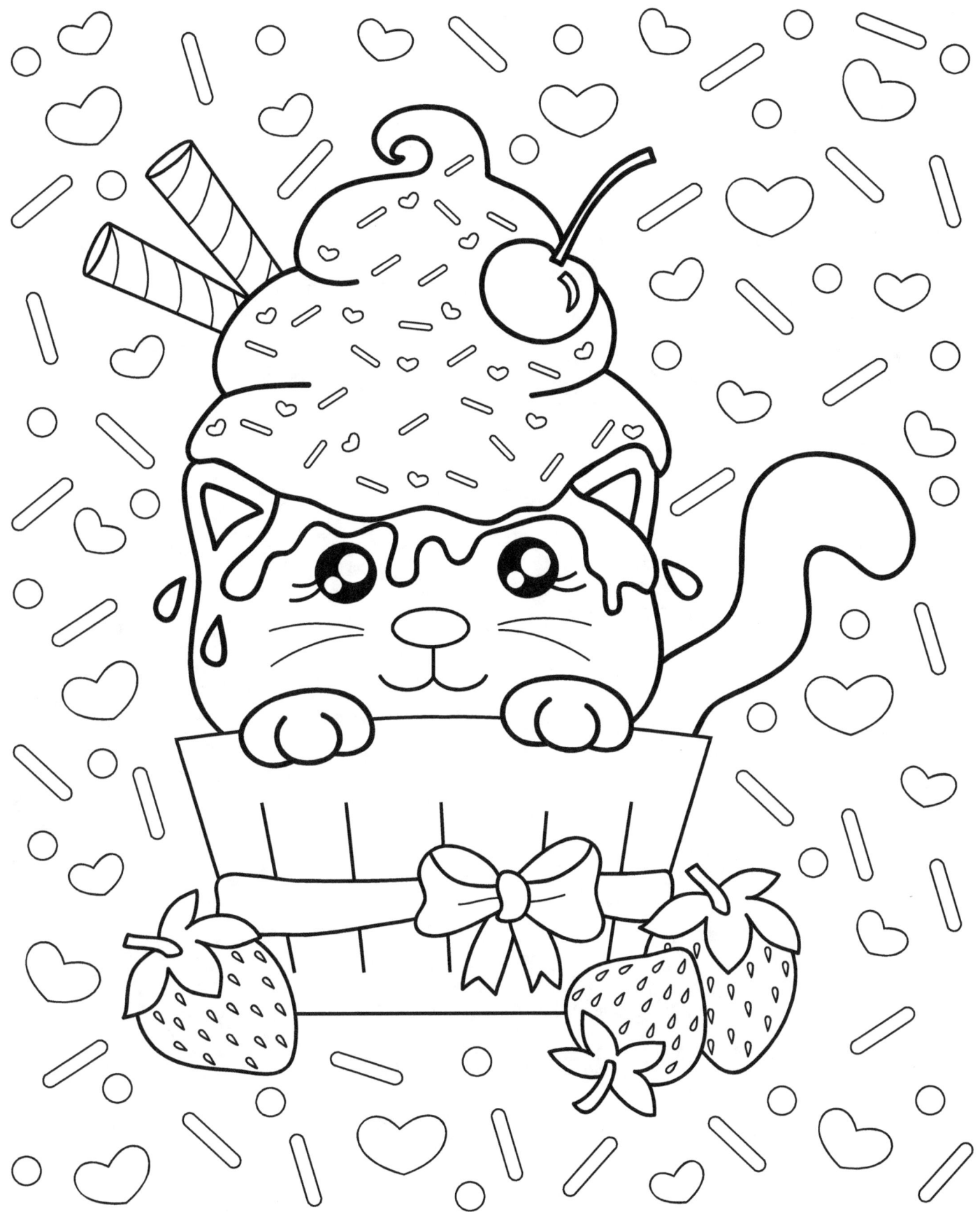

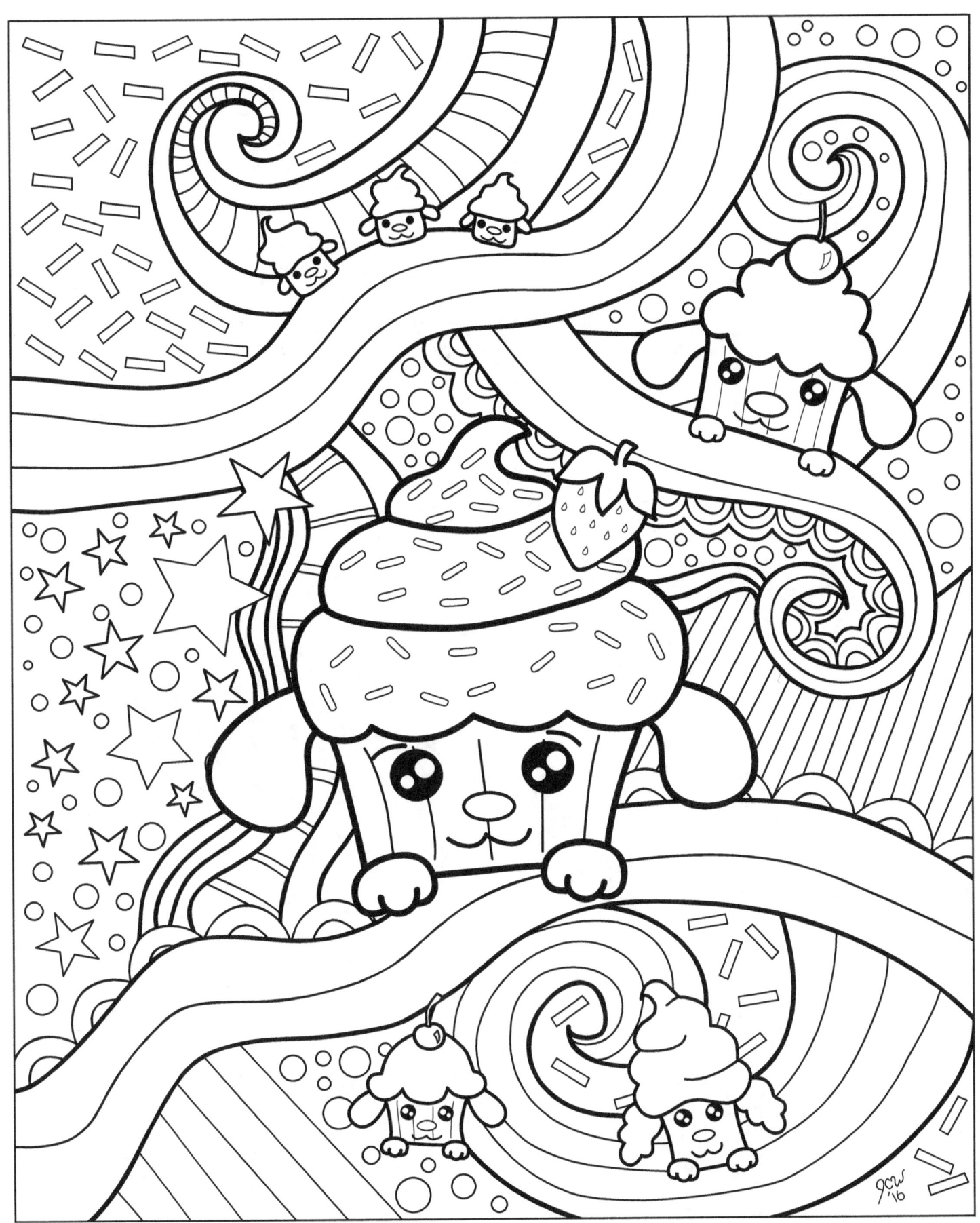

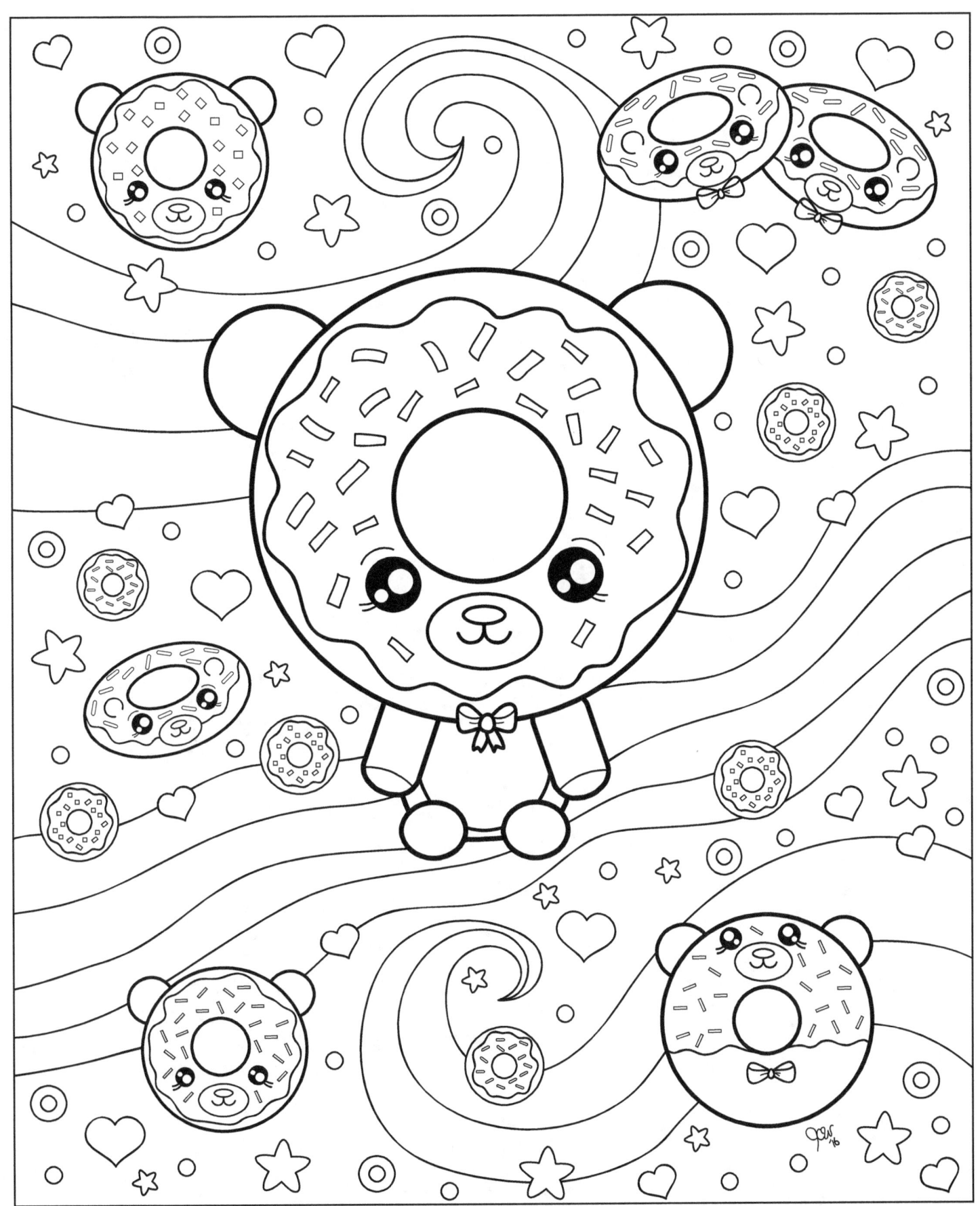

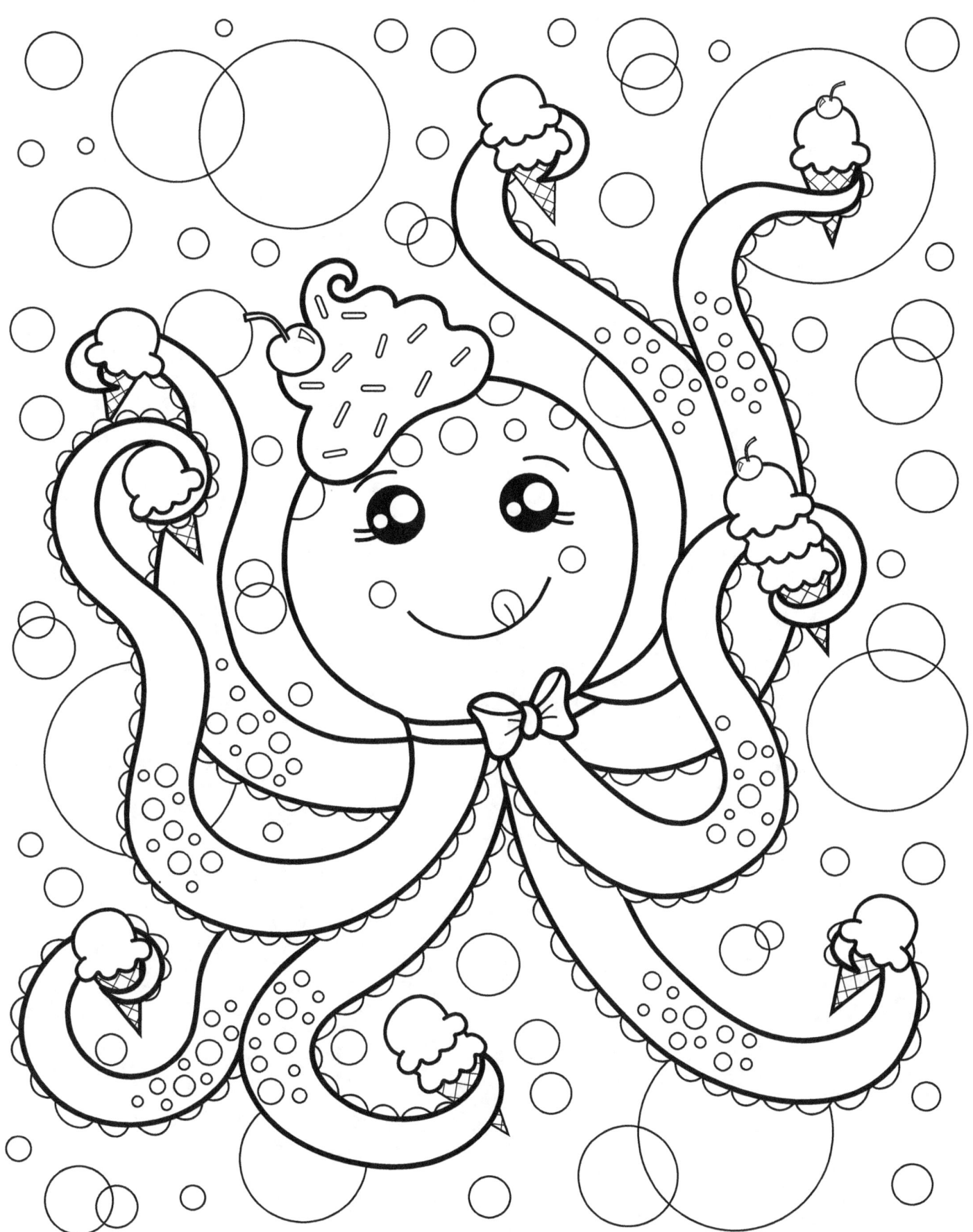

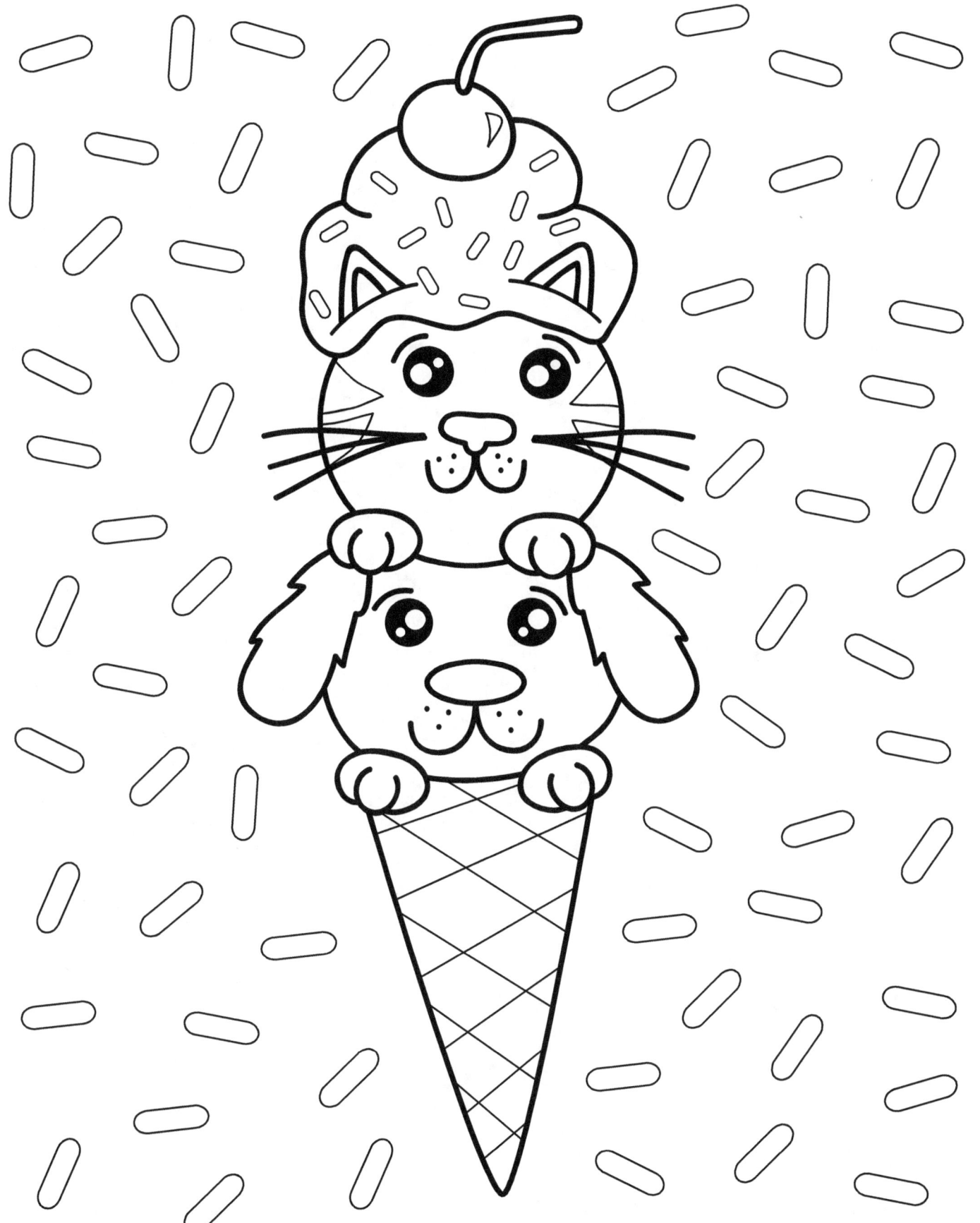

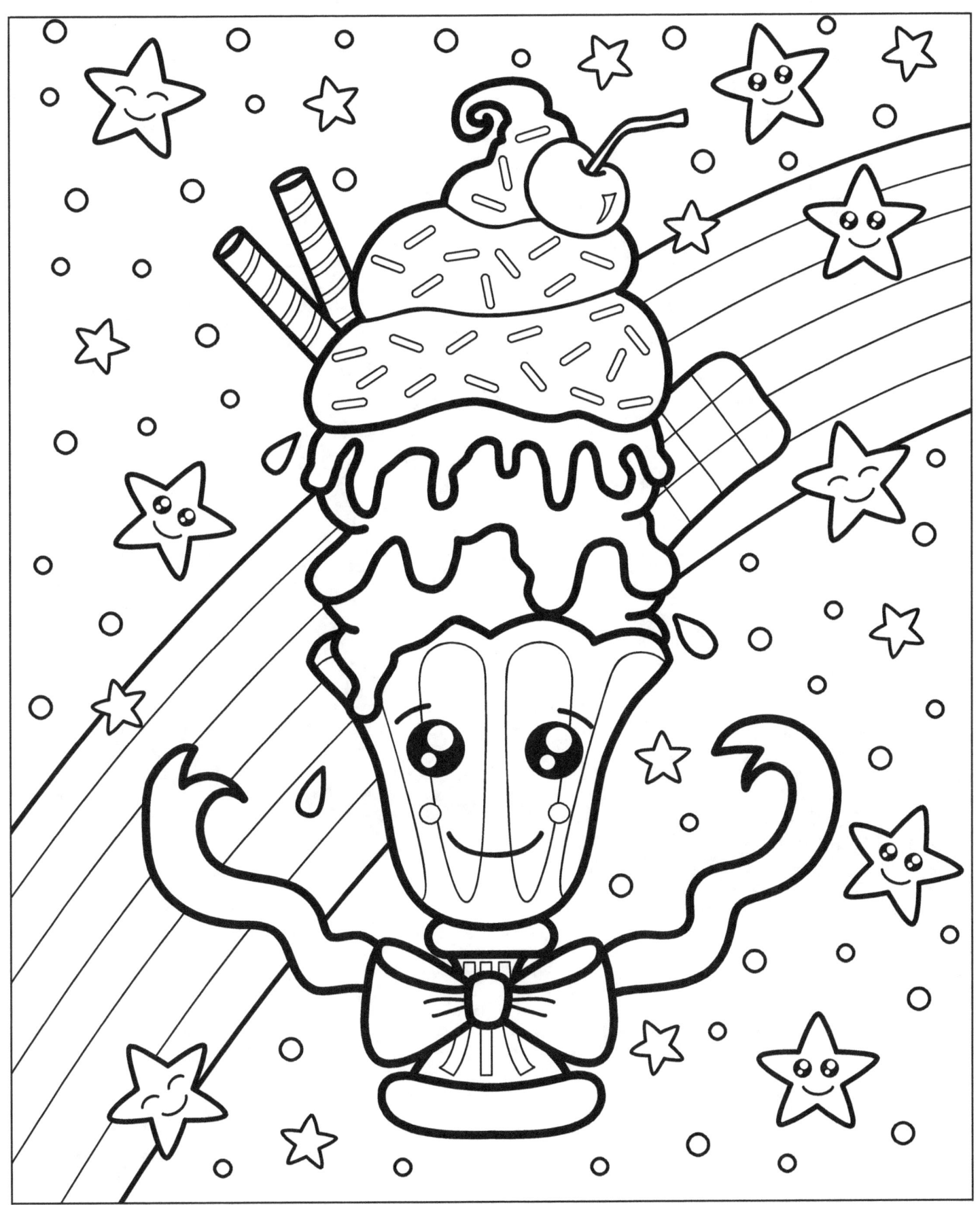

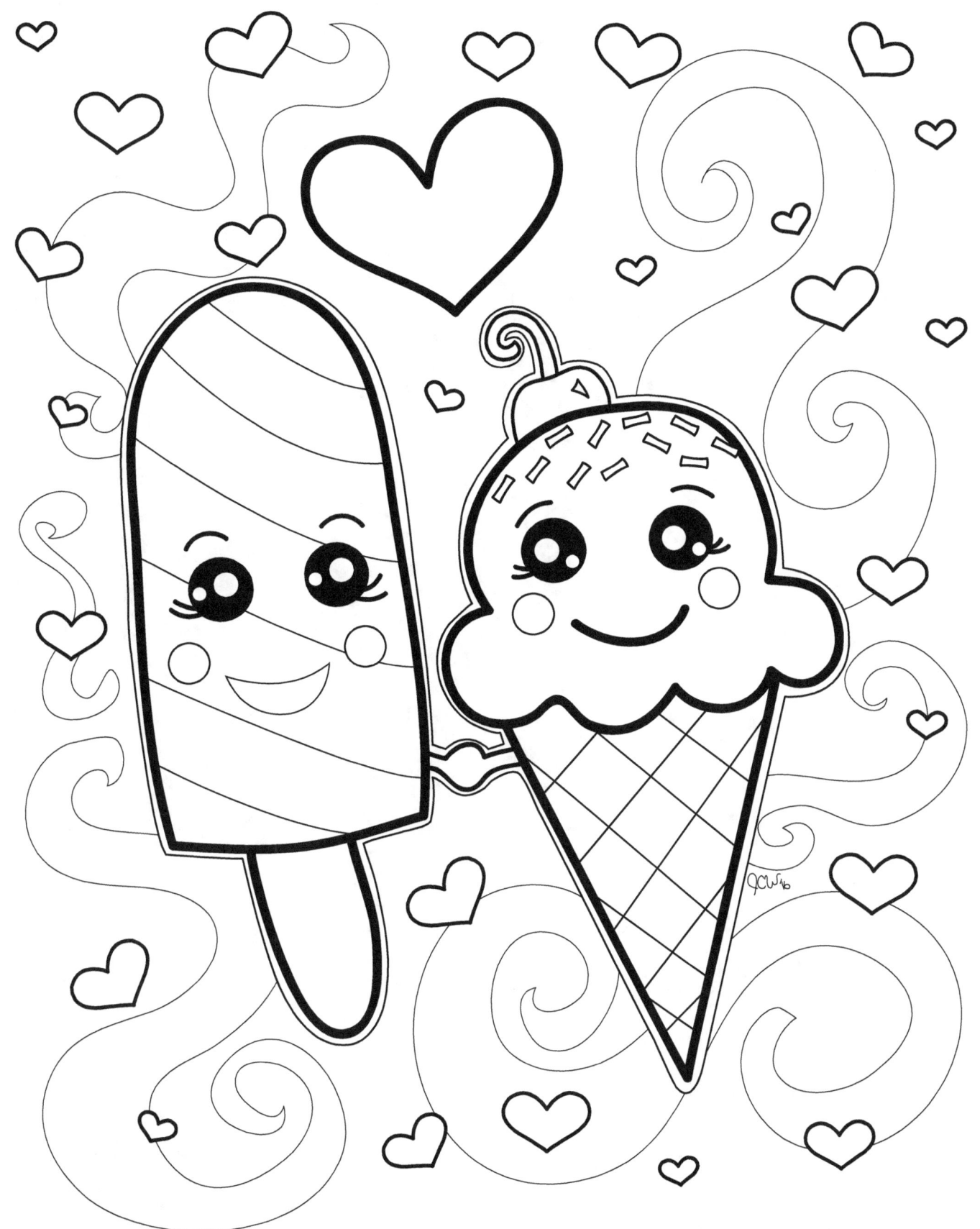

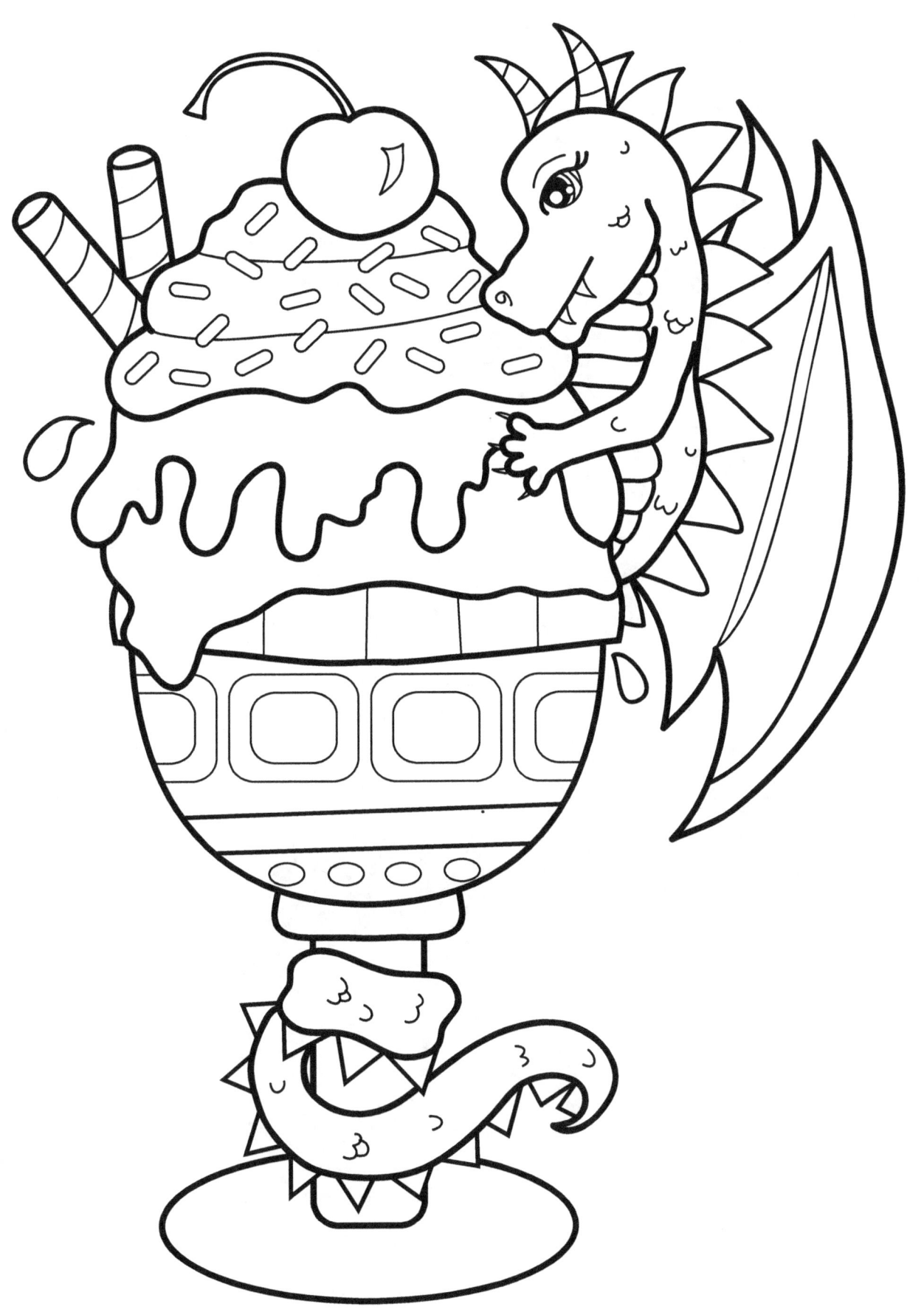

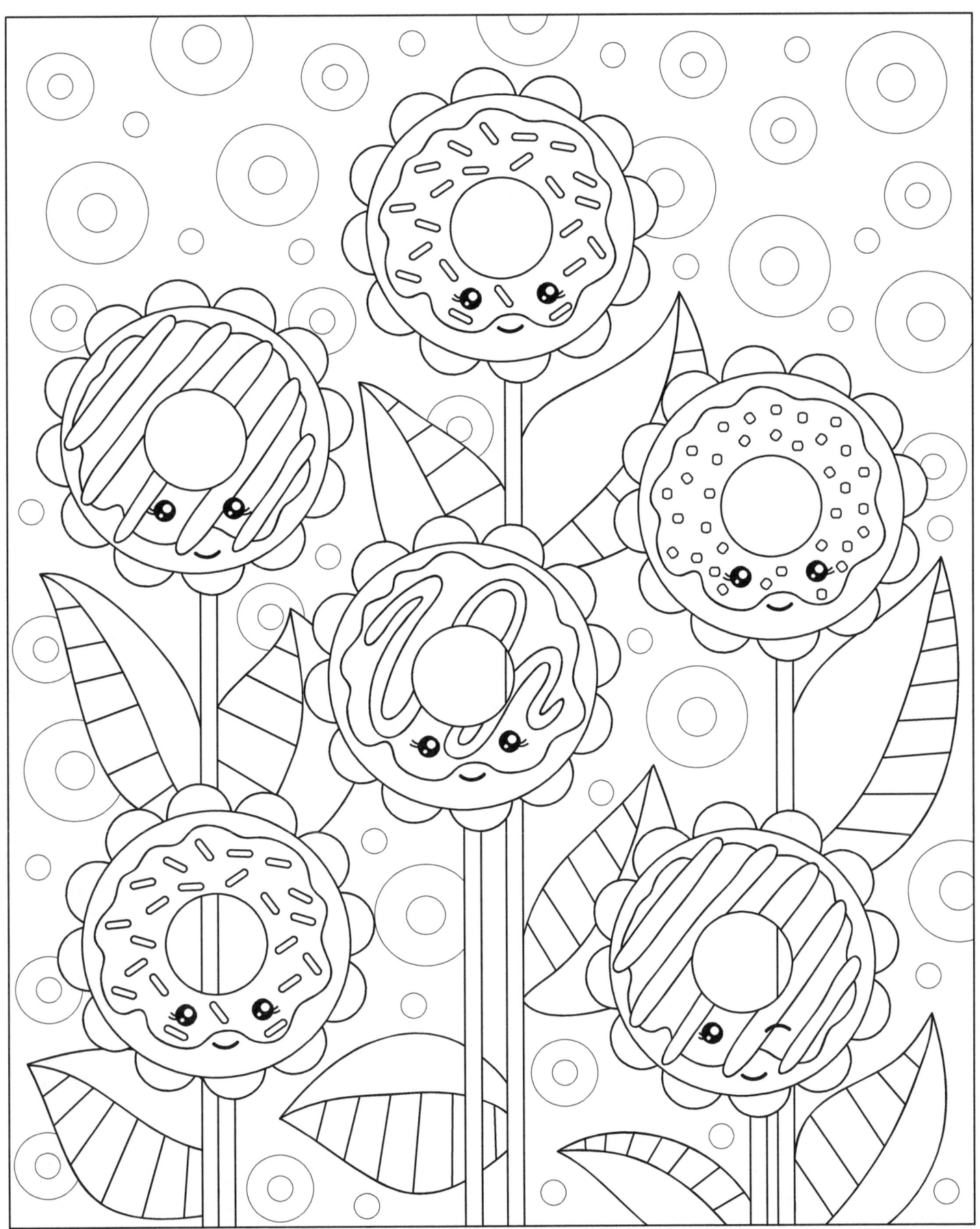

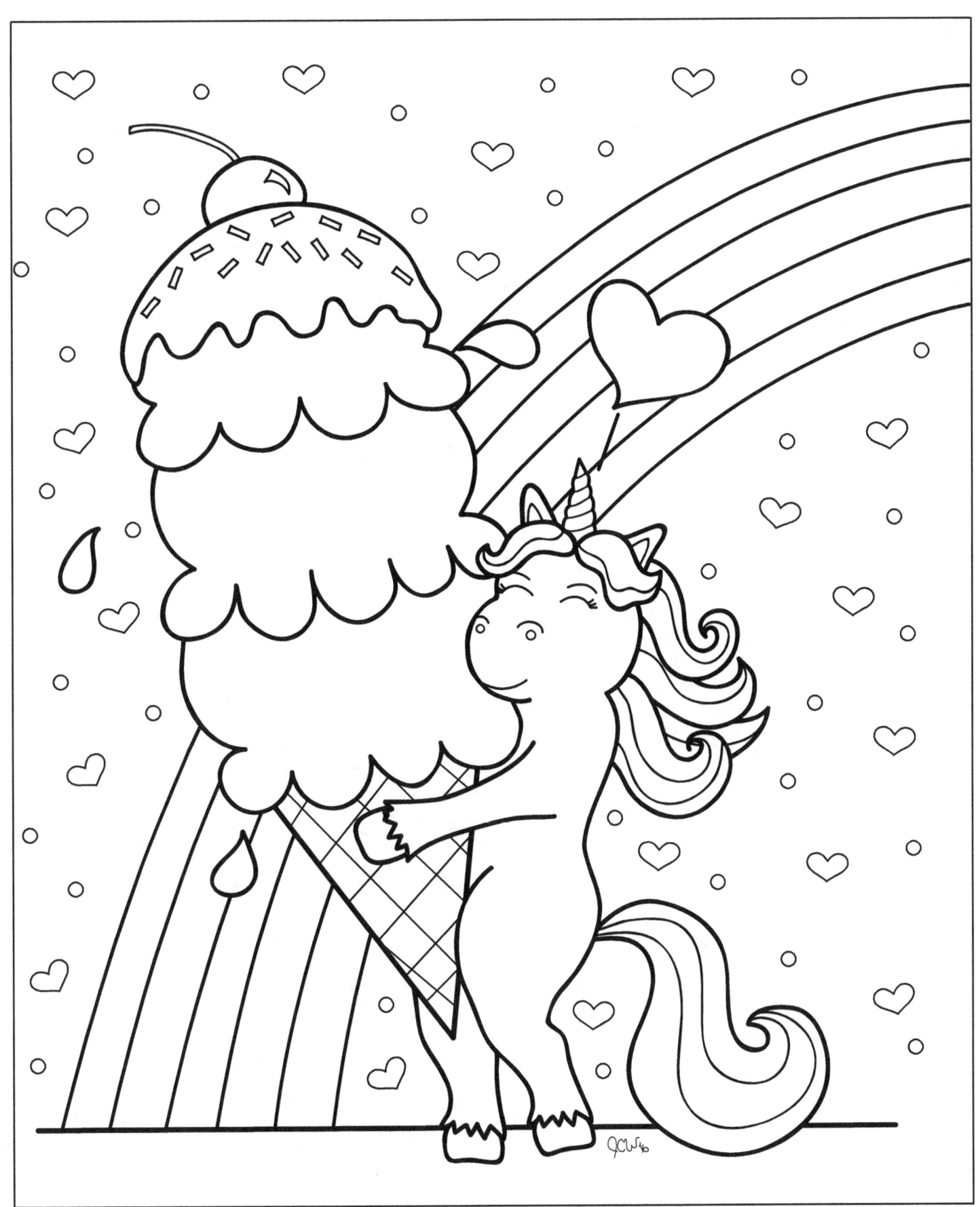

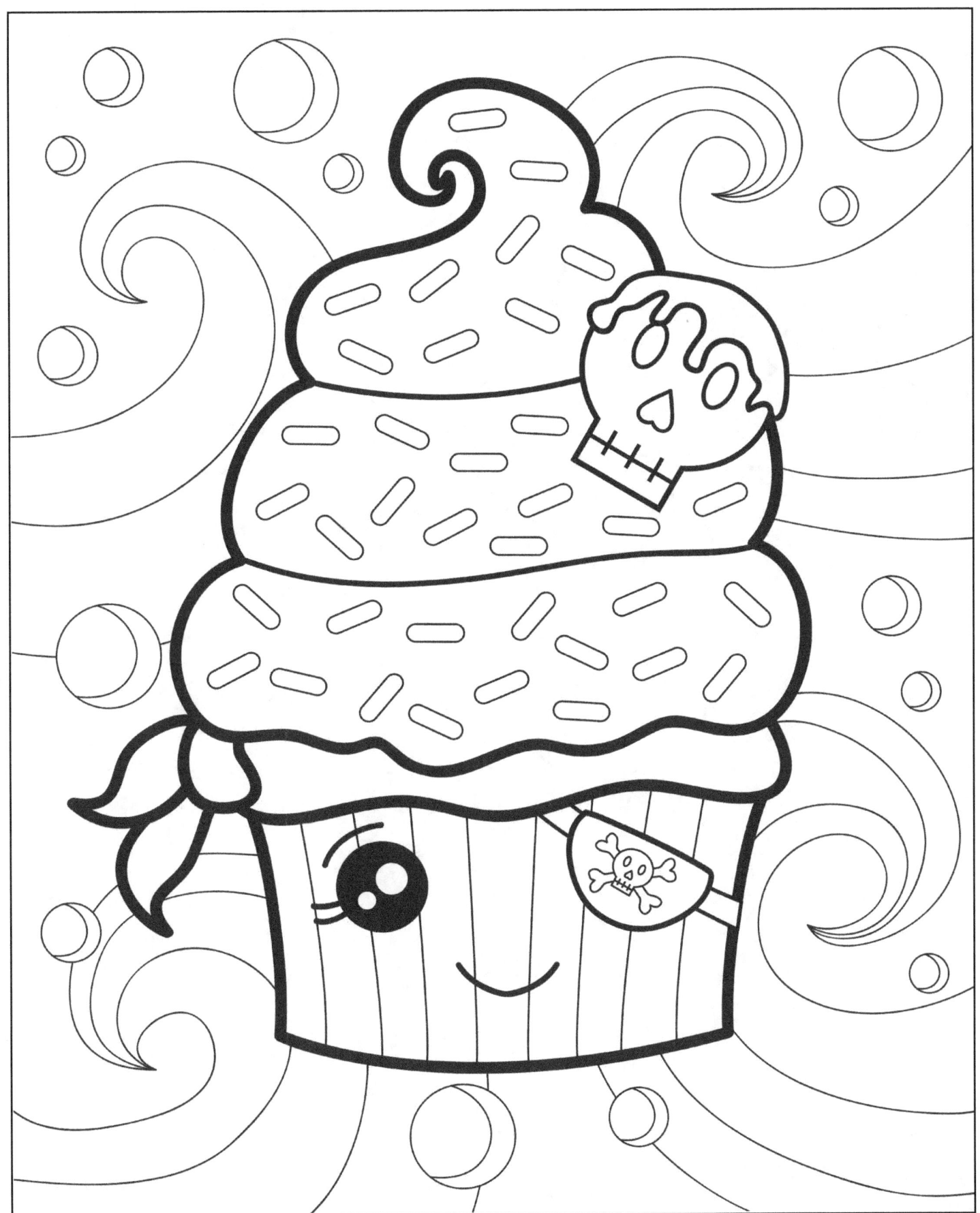

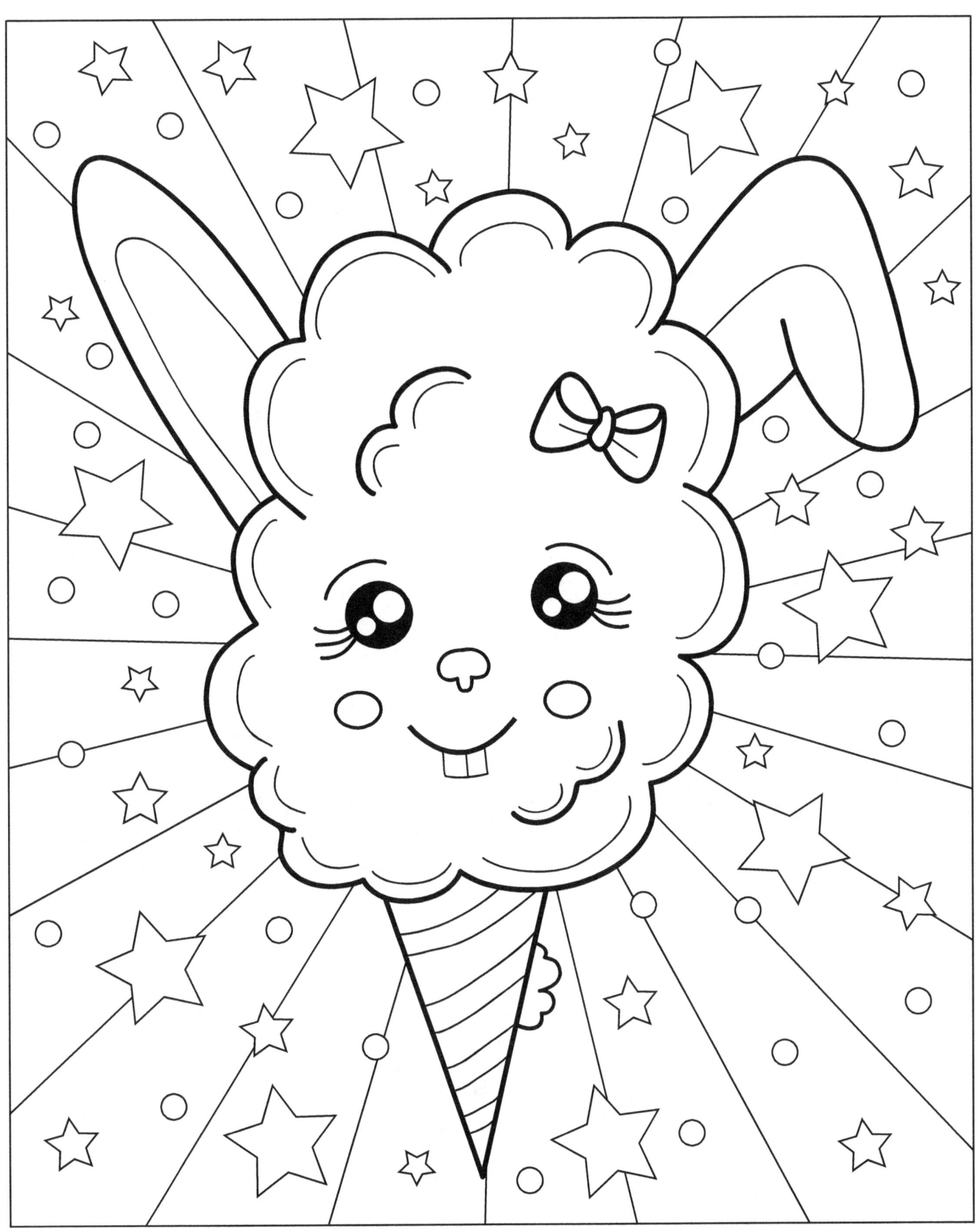

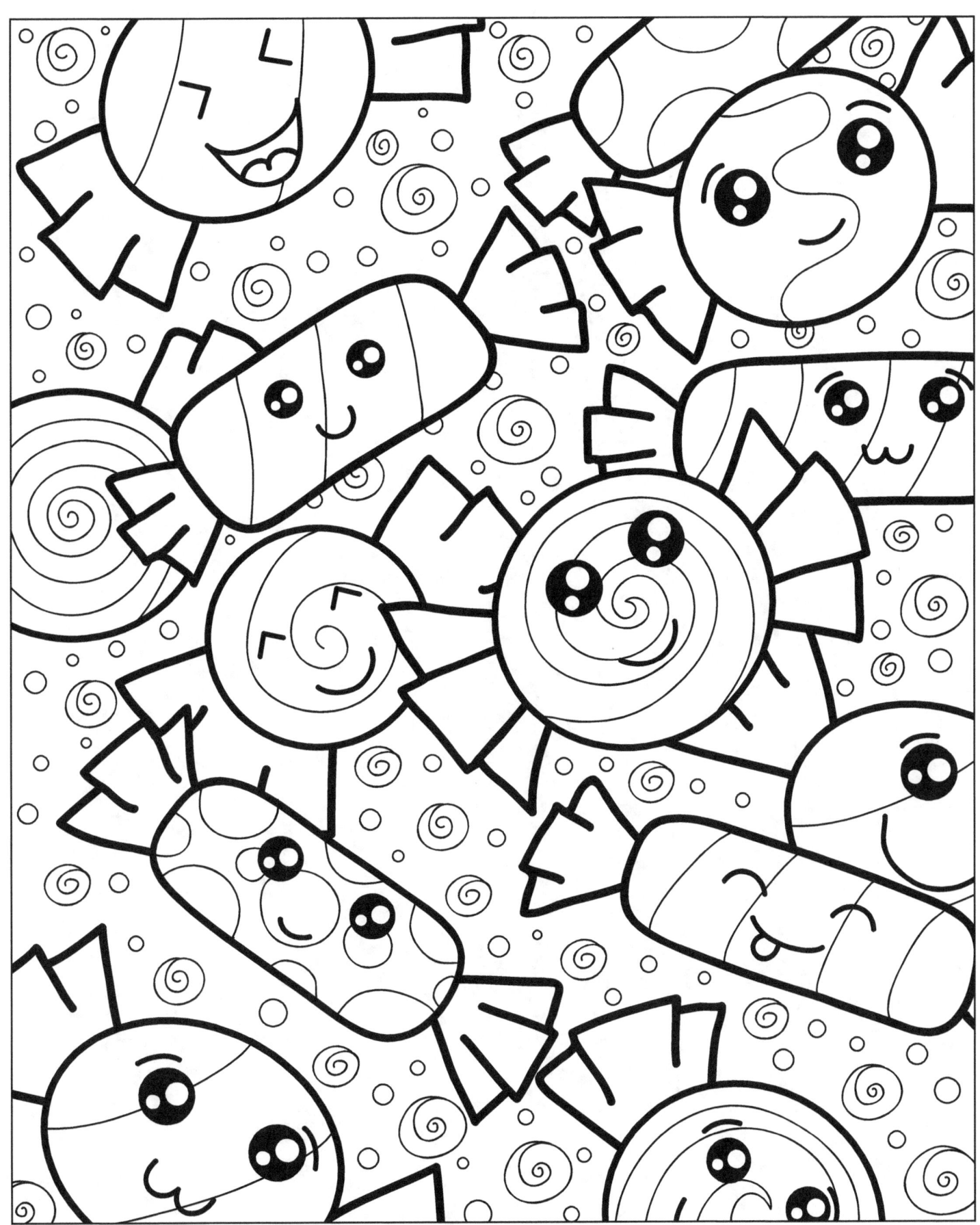

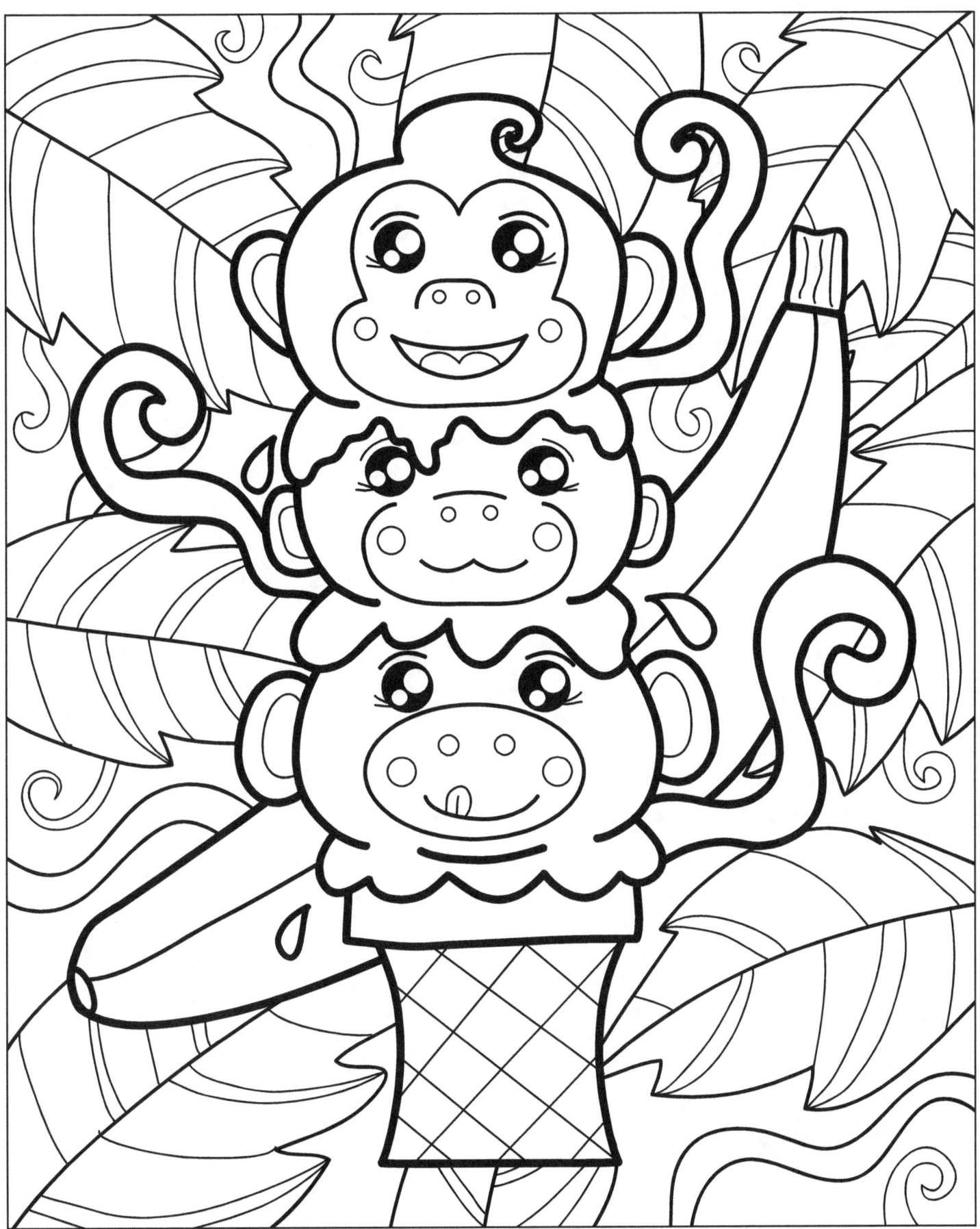

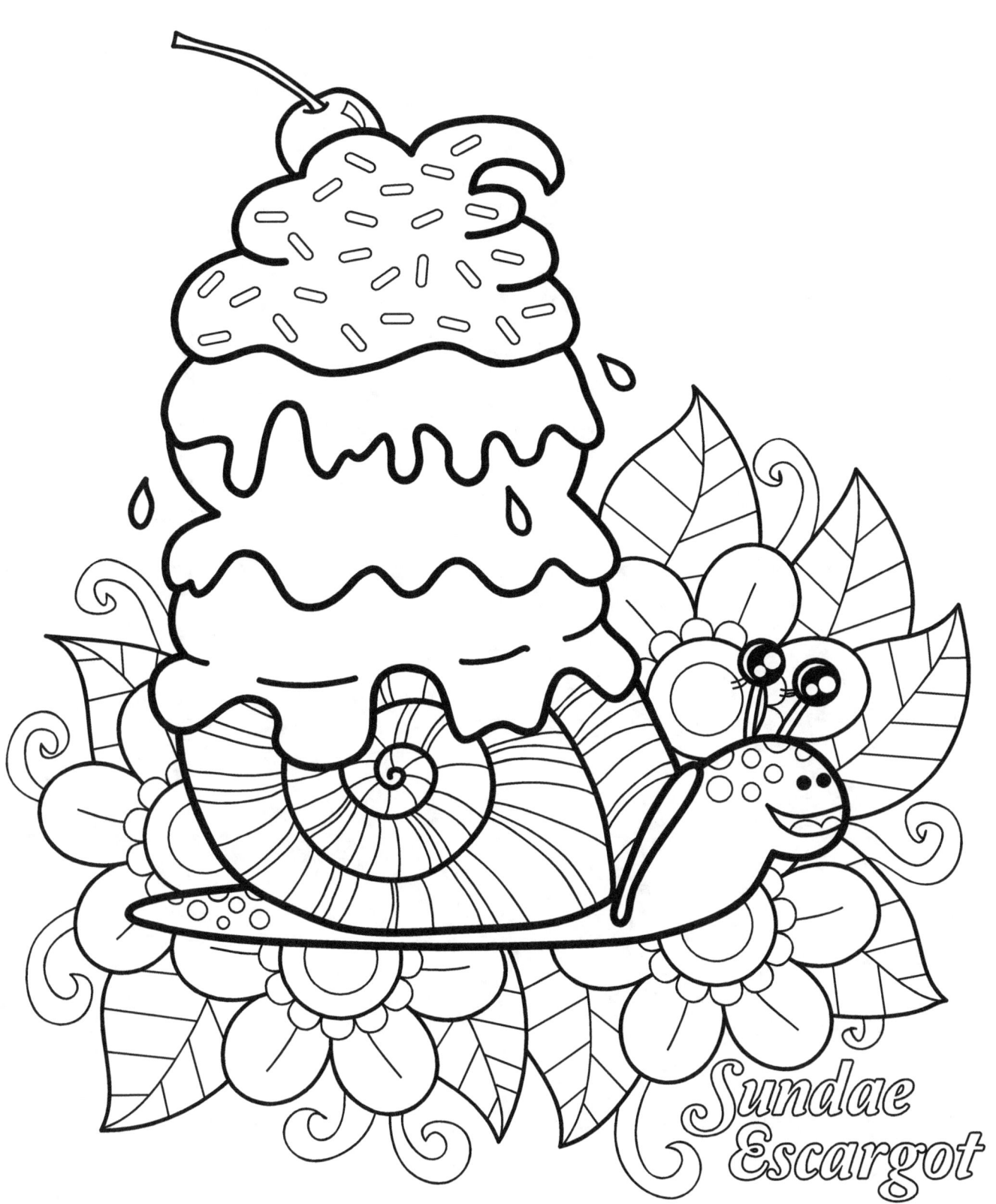

Sundae
Escargot

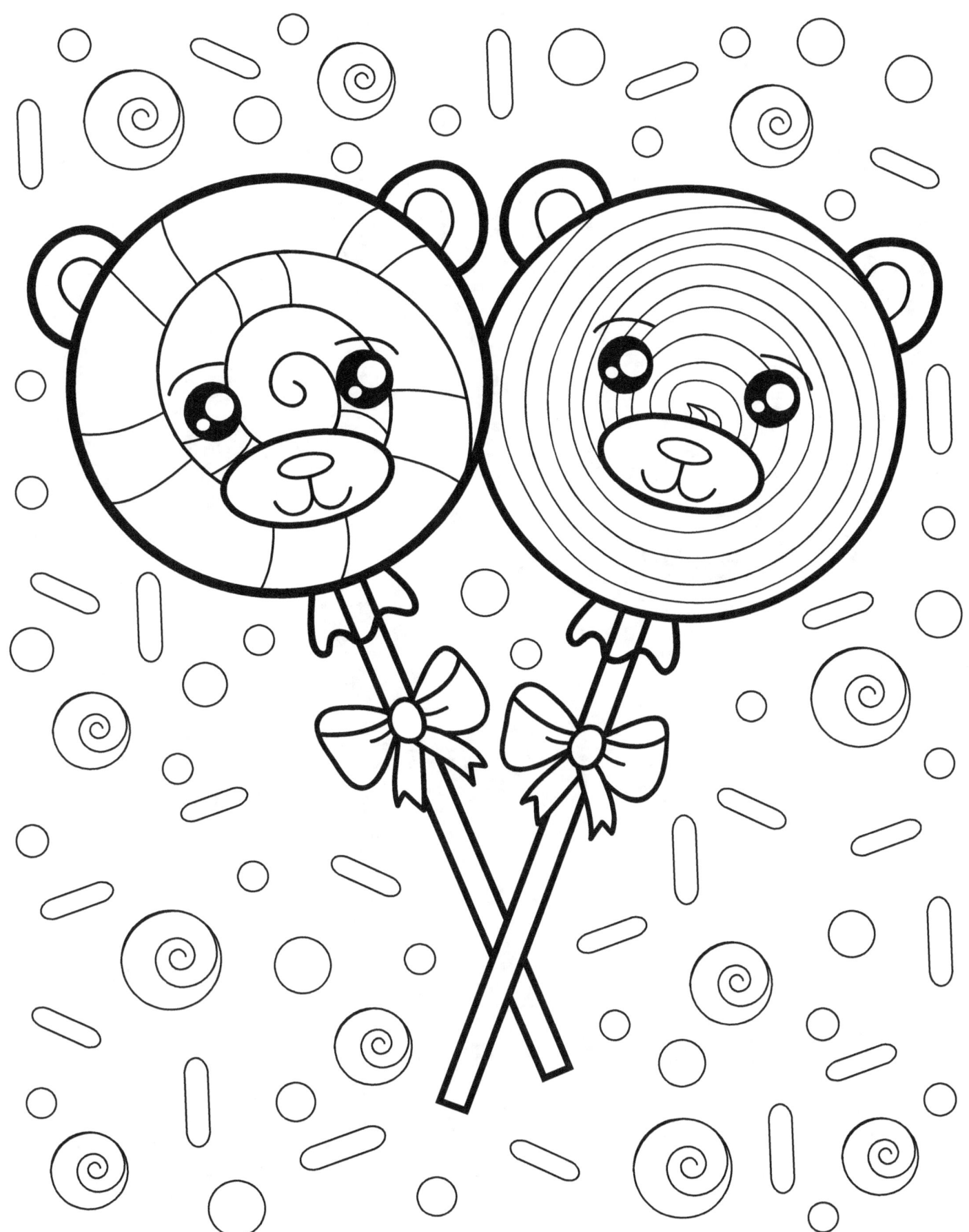

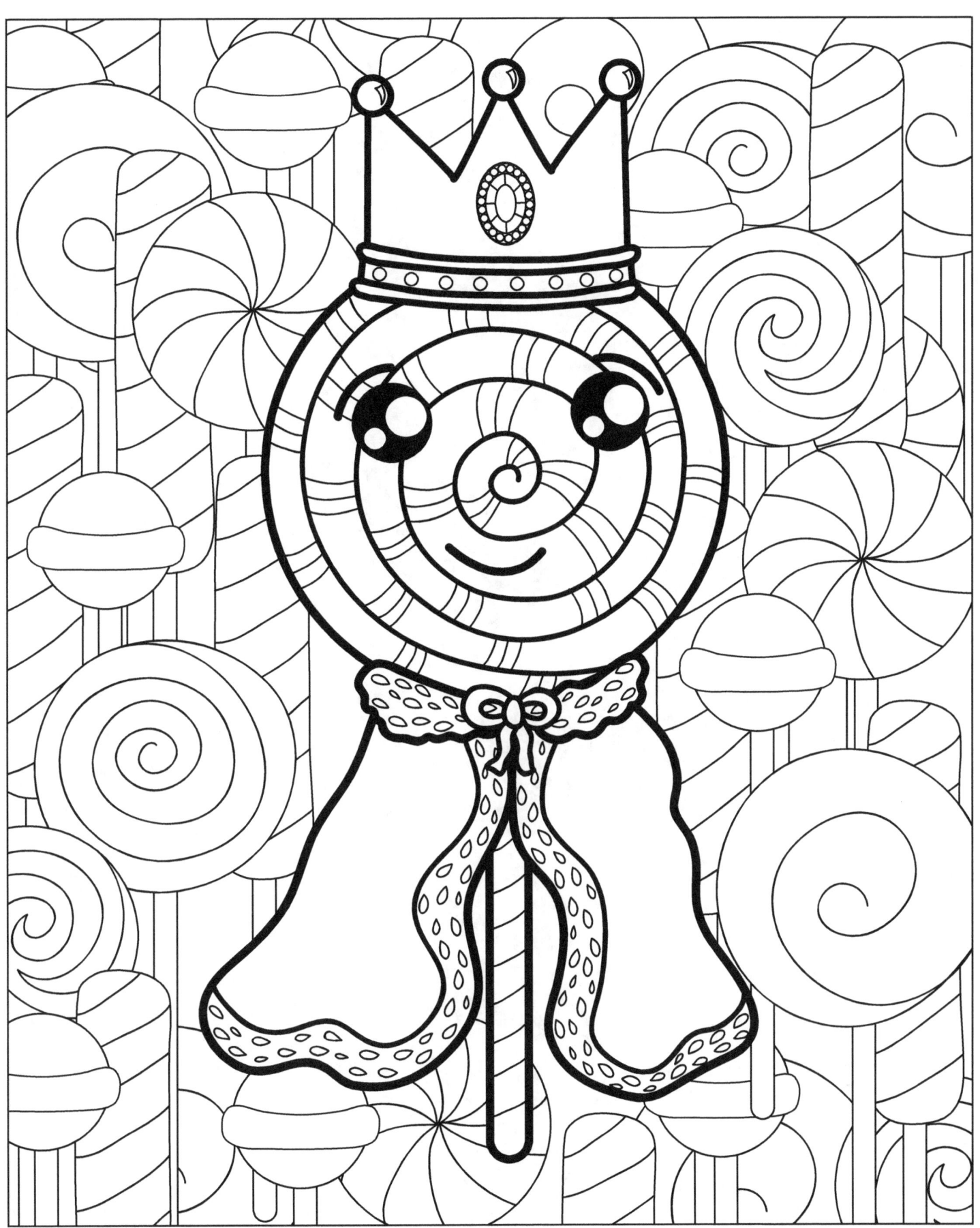

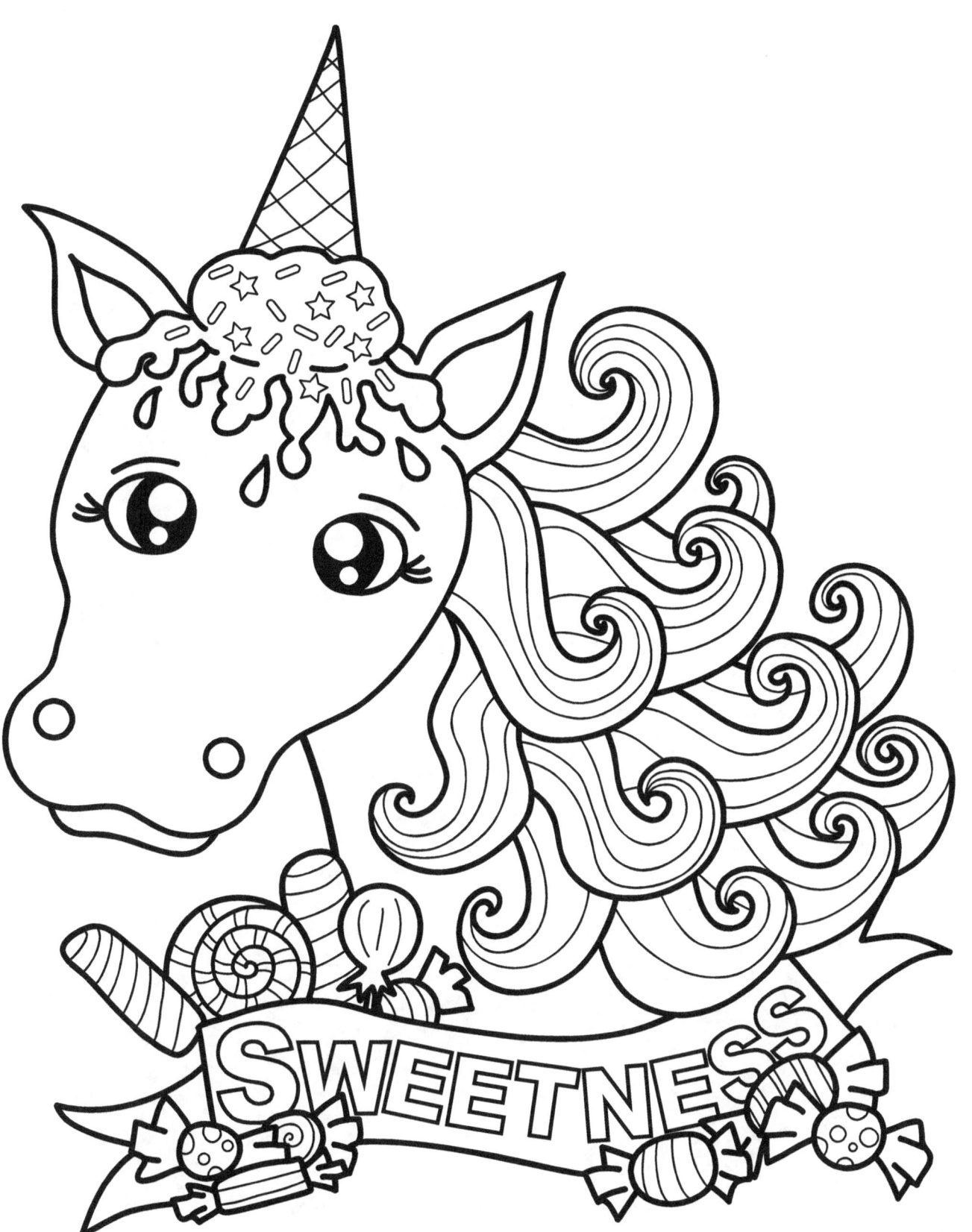

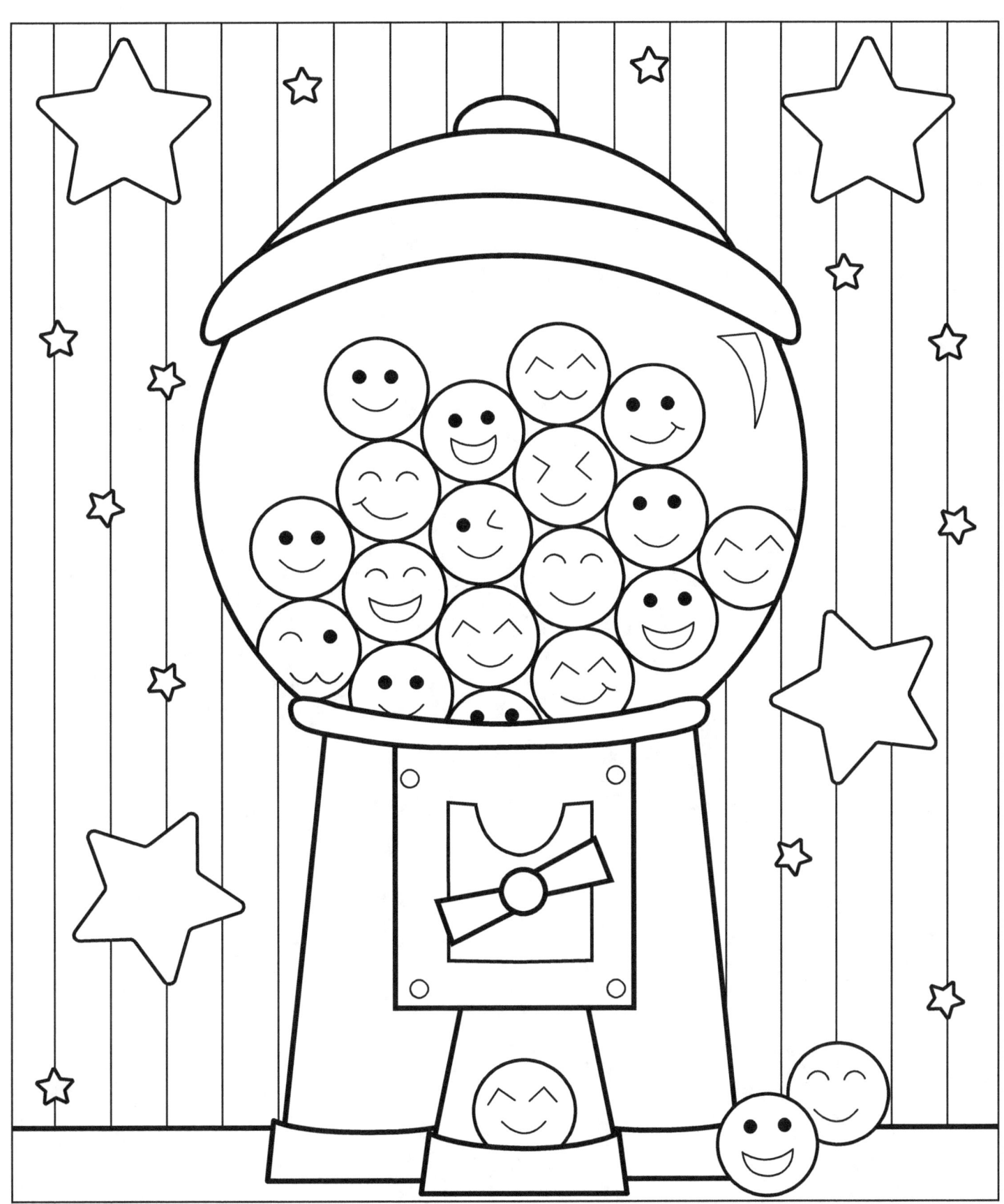

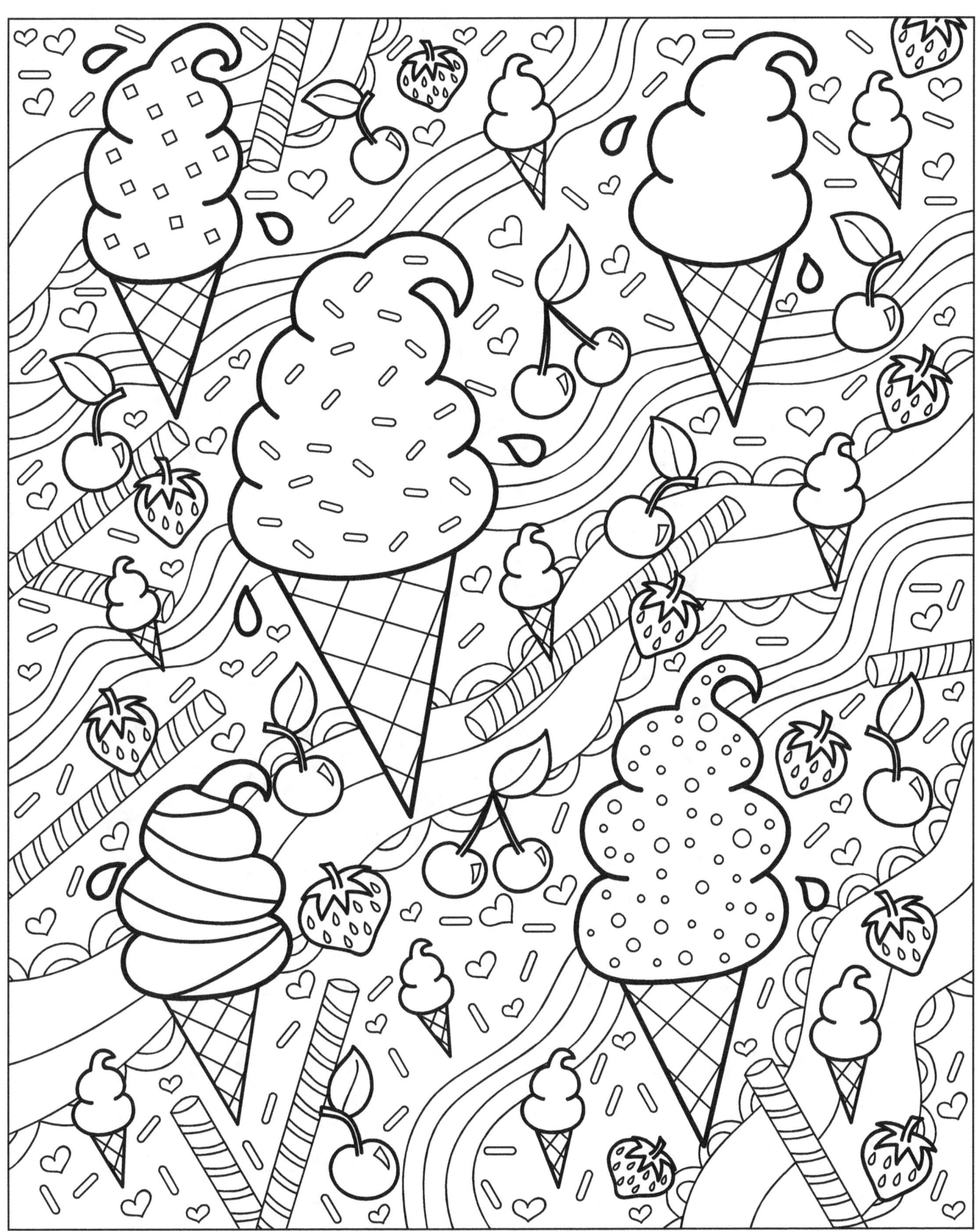

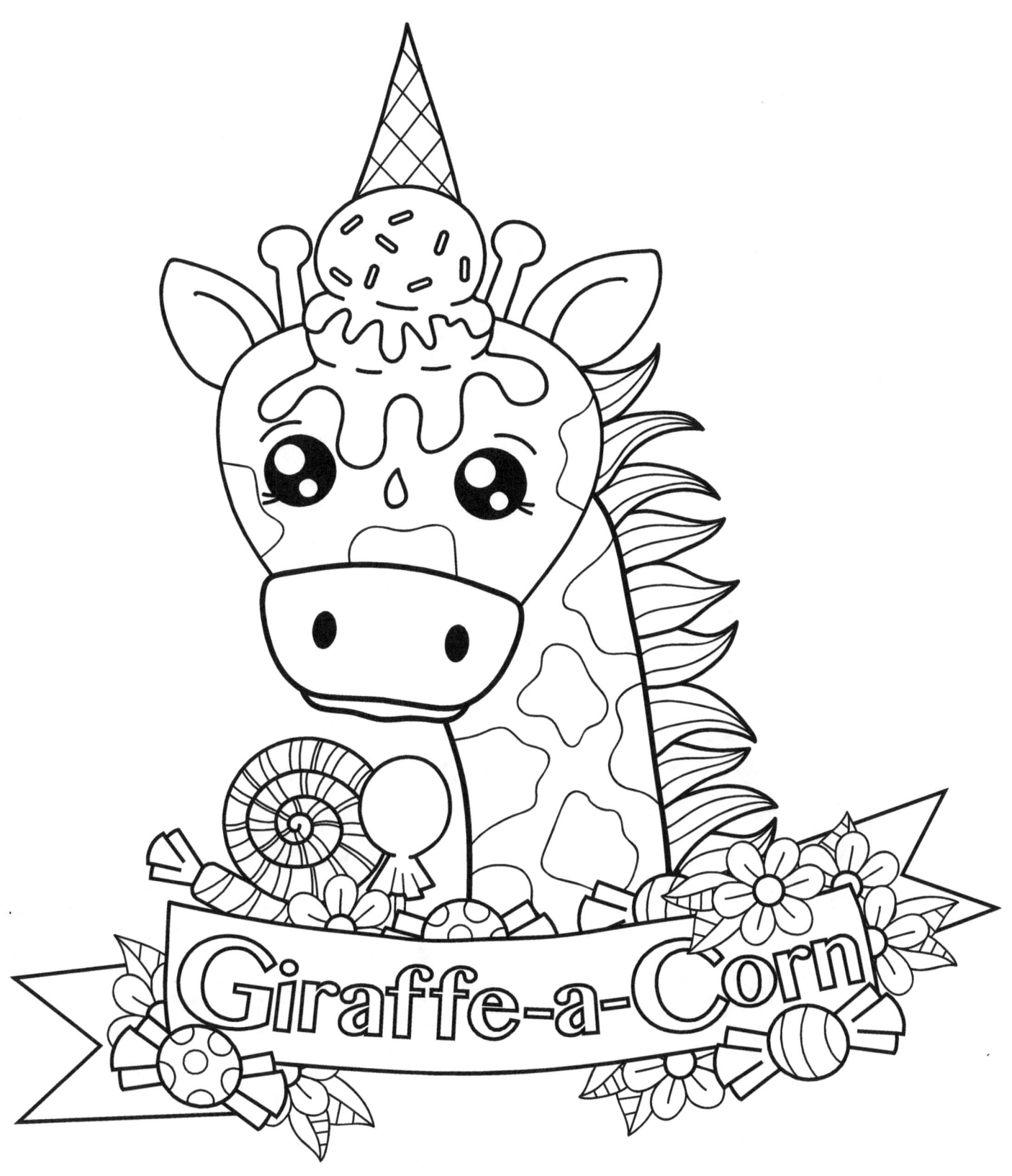

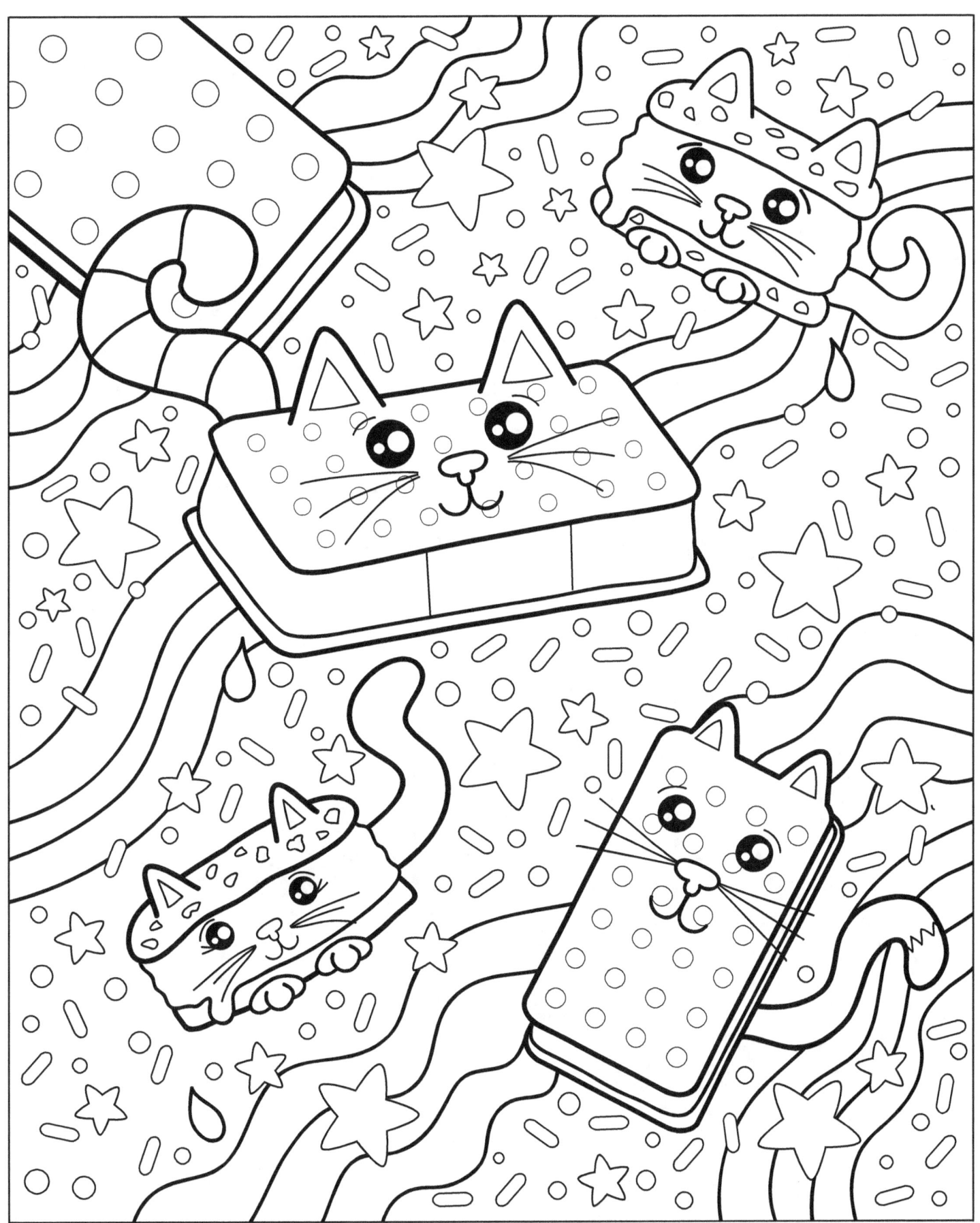

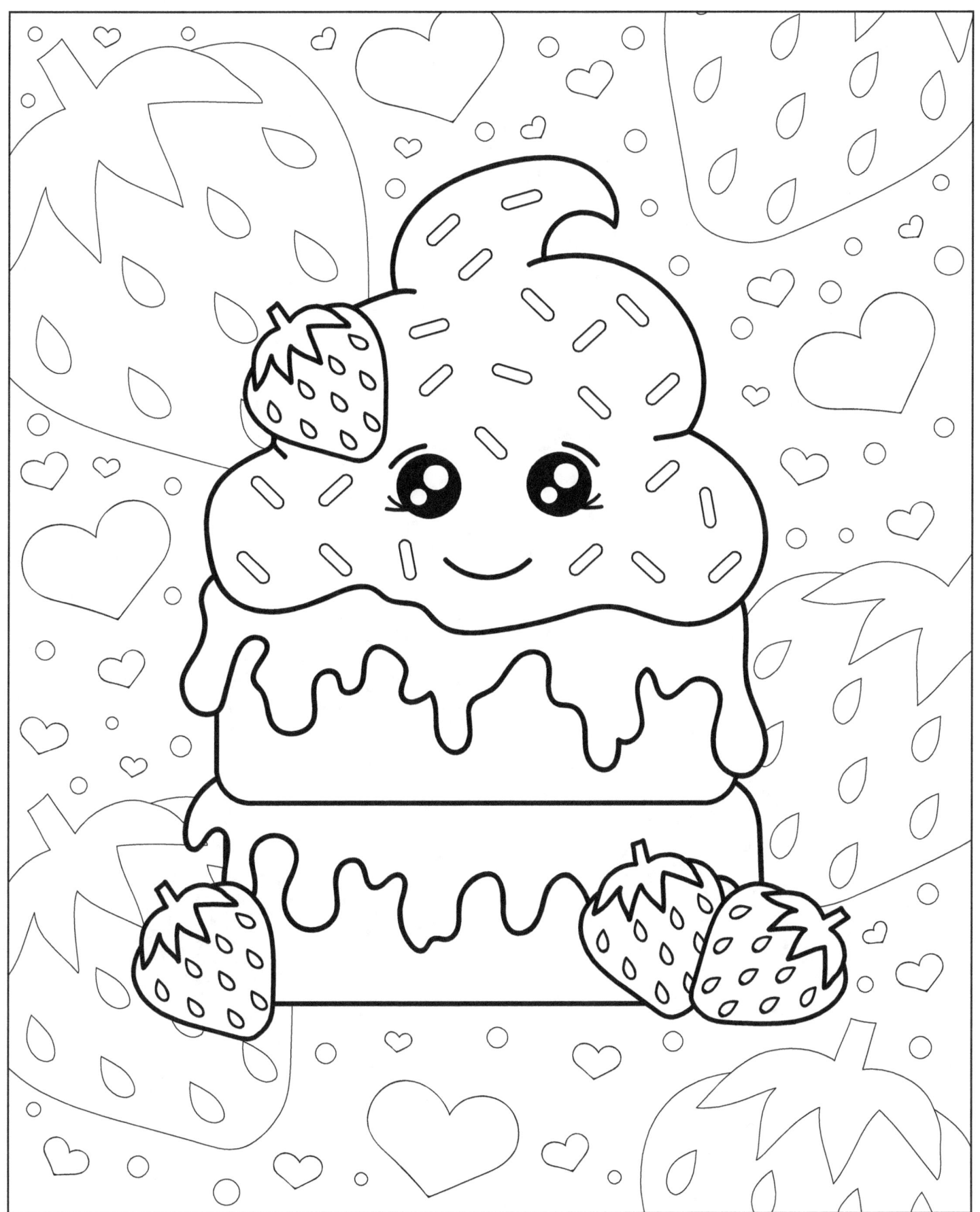

Check out my other books and
more on Amazon, Etsy, and
www.TheRootsOfDesign.com

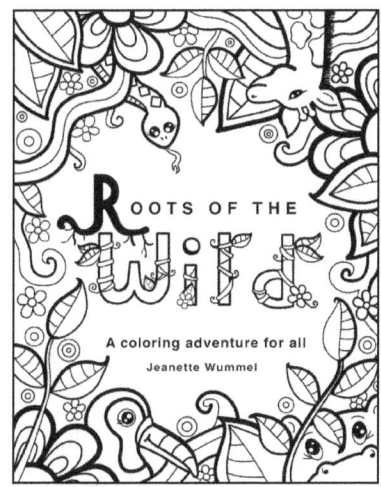
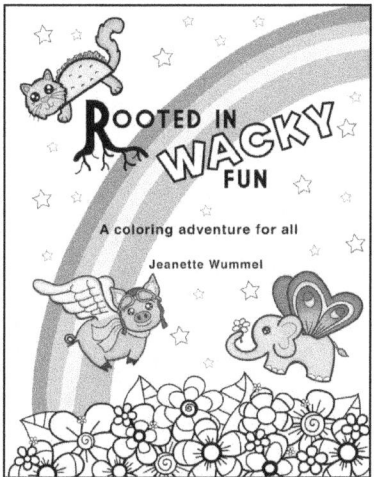
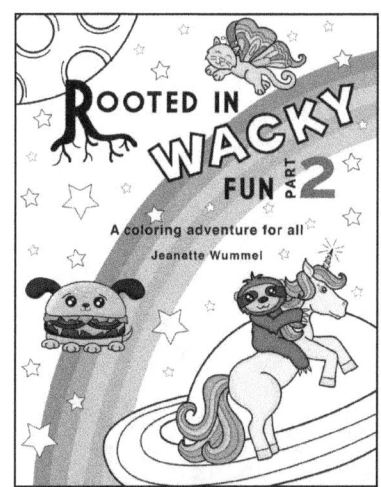
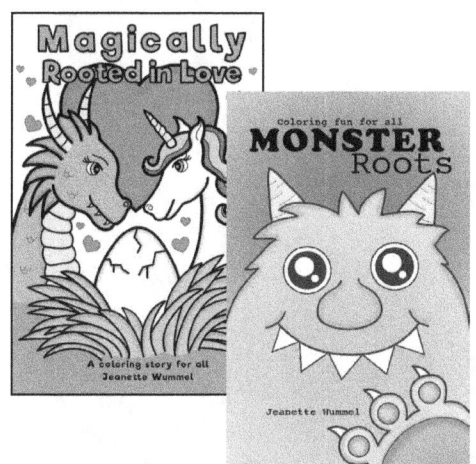
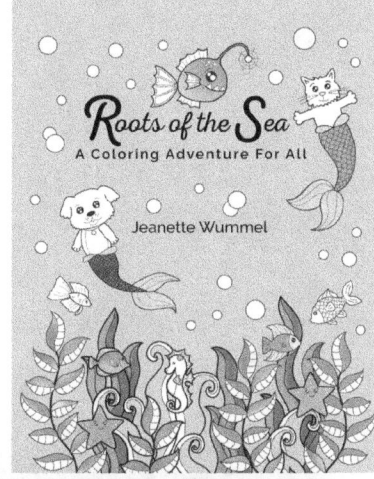
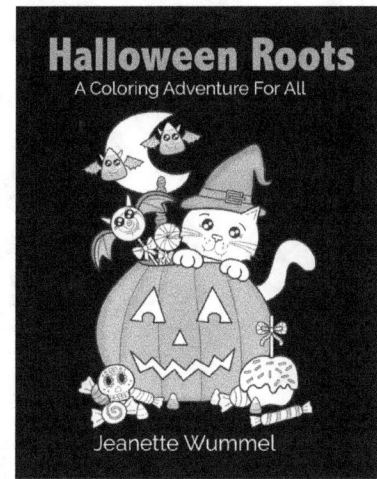
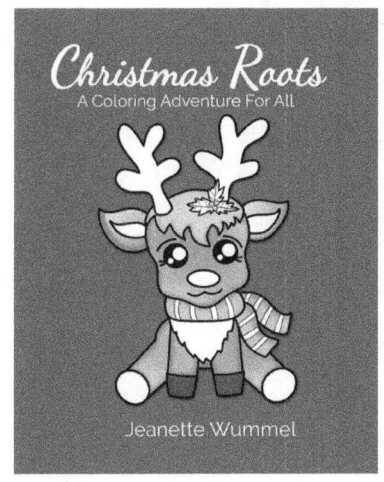
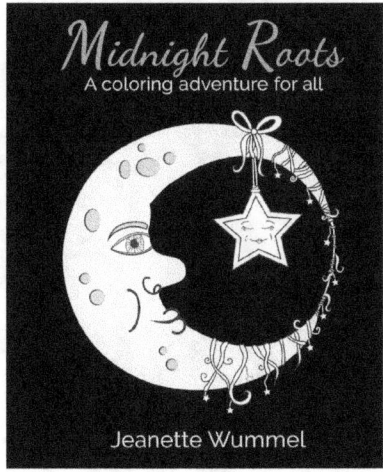
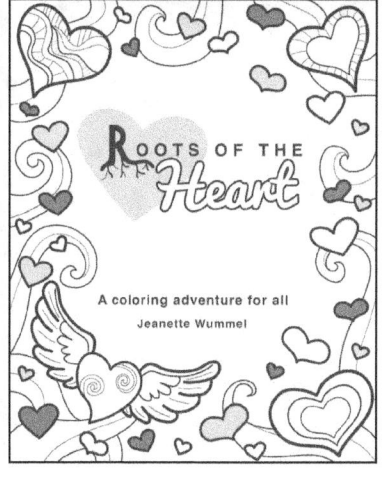